SYRIA

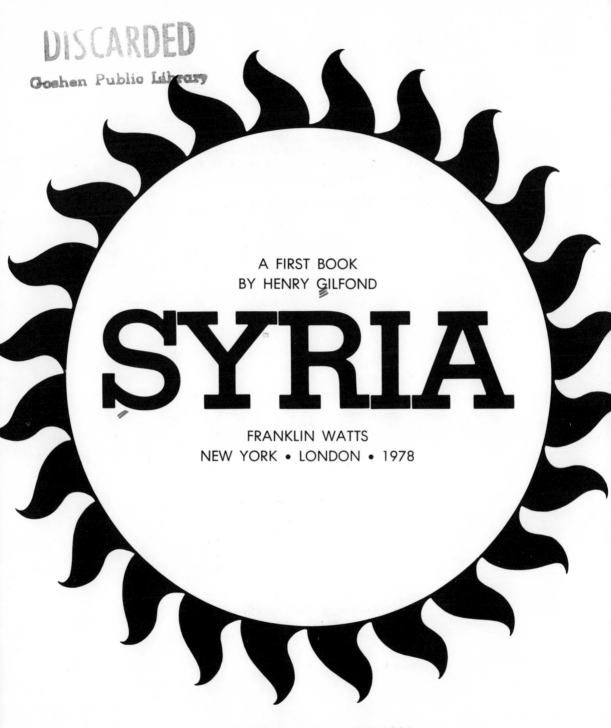

A FIRST BOOK
BY HENRY GILFOND

SYRIA

FRANKLIN WATTS
NEW YORK • LONDON • 1978

Cover design by Jackie Schuman

Photographs courtesy of:

Arab Information Center: pp. 11, 44; World Health Organization (photos by G. Nameh): pp. 14, 21, 33, 34; Eastfoto: p. 15; Novosti from Sovfoto: p. 26; United Nations: pp. 18, 38, 43; United Press International: p. 53.

Maps courtesy of: Vantage Art, Inc.

Library of Congress Cataloging in Publication Data

Gilfond, Henry.
     Syria.

     (A First book)
     Bibliography: p.
     Includes index.
     SUMMARY: Discusses the geography, his-
tory, culture, people, and present political problems of Syria with emphasis on the conflict with
neighboring Israel.
     1. Syria—Juvenile literature.   [1. Syria]
I. Title.
DS93.G54   956.91   78-9304
ISBN 0-531-02238-2

CONTENTS

TO PEACE ON EARTH

SYRIA

THE SYRIAN ARAB REPUBLIC

Syria is one of the oldest countries in the world. Its history goes back to biblical days, long before Abraham became the father of the Hebrew nation.

At one time Lebanon, most of Israel and Jordan, and sections of the Arabian Peninsula were part of Syria. Today the Syrian Arab Republic, as it is officially called, is just a little larger than 71,498 square miles (185,180 sq km).

A 104-mile (167-km) stretch of the Mediterranean Sea lies on its west. Along with the Mediterranean, Lebanon and Israel form Syria's western limits. On its north, 485 miles (782 km) of frontier separate Syria from Turkey. This is Syria's longest border with any sea or land mass. On its east and southeast lies Iraq. On its south, it is bordered by Jordan.

Many Syrians, and especially those who live in the border areas, consider the boundary lines with Iraq, Jordan, and Lebanon artificial. They look on all Arabs, wherever they live in the Middle East, as brothers. Syrian nomads called Bedouin completely ignore established border lines and regularly cross the frontiers of Jordan and Iraq to graze and water their flocks of sheep and goats.

But the attitude of the Syrians toward Turkey and Israel is quite different. Turkey and Israel are considered unfriendly nations, if not enemies. This holds particularly true for Israel. Since 1948, when Israel was established as an independent nation, Syria has fought a number of wars to remove Israel from what it considers to be Arab soil. The only result of all these efforts has been the loss to Israel of part of what was Syria's territory, the Golan Heights.

THE LAND

Syria is not a large country. The nature of its land, however, as well as of its climate, changes swiftly as one moves from west to east, or north to south. There are mountains and valleys in the northwest. In the middle of the country and in the southeast there are the wastelands of the Syrian Desert. In certain areas of the country, the people enjoy a mild Mediterranean climate. In other areas the winters are cold, and the summers very hot.

Except for along its humid Mediterranean coast, Syria gets very little rainfall. Its land is mostly dry. Its most arid regions get less than 4 inches (10 cm) of rain throughout the year. This lack of sufficient rainfall accounts for the condition of the greater part of Syria's soil, and for what grows on it. It also accounts for the kind of wildlife that is to be found in Syria.

(2)

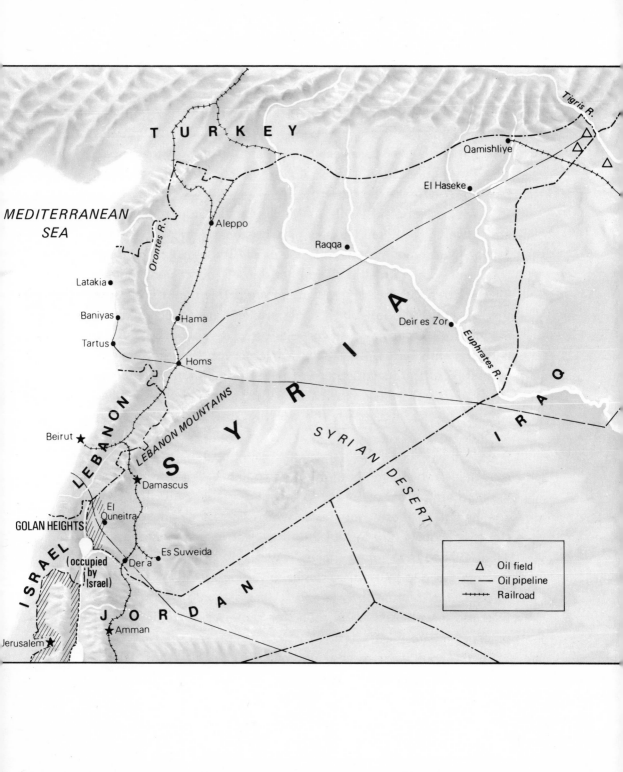

Generally, Syria is divided into five regions. There is the Mediterranean coastal strip, with the mountains behind it, in the northwest. There is the central plain which stretches from the city of Homs to the city of Aleppo, then east to the Euphrates River. There is the southwestern area around the city of Damascus; the northeastern plains along the Euphrates River, and beyond; and finally the desert.

The coastal plain along the Mediterranean is narrow. It is an area covered with sand dunes and broken by the hills of the Jabal al-Nusayriya Mountains to the east. Although this region of Syria gets some rainfall and is rather densely populated, there is little agricultural development in the area. This may be because the Alawites, who inhabit this coastal plain, are a poor minority among the Syrians. Whatever the case, its seaports, Latakia, Baniyas, and Tartus, are fairly active towns though most of Syria's exports are shipped out of Beirut and Tripoli in Lebanon. There are other smaller towns and villages along the coastline where, for the most part, the Alawites make their living by fishing.

To the east of the Syrian coastal plain, the Jabal al-Nusayriya Mountains, which are about 40 miles (64 km) wide, stretch from the northern border of Turkey to Lebanon on the south. The average height of these mountains, which consist chiefly of limestone, is about 4,000 feet (1,220 m). Near its Lebanon end, the Jabal al-Nusayriya range makes way for the Hom Gap. It was through this gap that, for centuries, invading armies moved their forces to the interior of Syria and farther east into Asia. The gap was also a well-used trade route for camel caravans in ancient times, as it is to this day.

To the southwest of the mountains is the Hawran plateau.

Many centuries ago the plateau was fertile land, excellent for farming. Today much of the plateau is covered with ancient lava deposits, the result of past earthquakes. Great blocks of broken, disintegrated lava make any use of the land difficult if not impossible.

Central and southeastern Syria is largely desert land. However, a part of Syria lies in the Fertile Crescent, an area that is watered by the Euphrates and Tigris rivers. This area of the country, called the Jazira region, provides Syria with most of its food. It is the area in which almost half of Syria's people live. It is in this region that Syria has built its most important cities (except for Damascus, its capital and largest city).

VEGETATION

The climate of any country affects its landscape. It also helps shape the nature of things that grow on its land as well as the animals, birds, and insects that live there.

More than 40 percent of the land of Syria is a yellow sandy or clayish semidesert soil. Nothing grows on this soil except a grass that is suitable only for grazing the sheep and goats of the Arab nomads.

Mediterranean scrubs such as brushwood, buckthorn, and tamarisk cover many of the slopes of Syria's mountains. Reed grass is found in the swamps. Anemones, poppies, irises, and other quick-growing and fragrant flowers grow in many parts of the country.

Rich, black soil covers only about 300,000 acres (121,458 hectares) of Syria, in the northeast. This region, Jazira, produces much of the wheat and cotton for Syrian consumption and manu-

facture. It is also an area in which deposits of oil and petroleum have been discovered.

Wheat is grown, too, in the humid coastal plain of Syria. Other important food crops grown in this region are barley, millet, corn, onions, garlic, cucumbers, tomatoes, and potatoes. The region also produces apples, figs, olives, dates, oranges, and other fruits.

There are some forests in northern Syria. Here one may find patches of Aleppo pine and smaller clusters of oak. Poplars, willows, and alders grow in the valleys of Syria. More common to much of Syria are olive, carob, and fruit trees. As one approaches the plateaus and semidesert lands of central and eastern Syria, however, trees slowly disappear. Only coarse shrubs and pasture grasses can survive in these areas.

WILDLIFE

Semidesert land is where camel herders take their flocks to graze and to seek water. But animals, insects, and birds live freely not only in the semidesert country but in the deserts as well. Antelopes and gazelles roam through the arid land. So do lizards, chameleons, and vipers. Wolves are occasionally sighted in mountainous areas. Deer, wildcats, porcupines, squirrels, hedgehogs, ermines, marten, rats, and mice are to be found almost everywhere in Syria.

Pelicans and flamingos live in the marshes of Syria, and eagles, owls, partridge, and vultures are common to the Syrian skies.

Among the more common insects that make their home in Syria are mosquitoes, sand flies, and grasshoppers. There are locusts, too, in Syria, and every now and then they prove to be a severe problem for the farmers and fruit growers. Locusts can destroy, and have destroyed, entire crops. The Syrian farmers, who can never produce too much because of the nature of the soil and the scarcity of water for irrigation, cannot afford even the occasional horde of locusts that comes their way.

SYRIAN CITIES: A BLEND OF OLD AND NEW

Damascus on the Barada River, Aleppo in the northwest, Homs on the Orontes River in the west, and Hama on the Orontes River in the north, are Syria's largest and most important cities. They are all ancient although all have developed as industrial and commercial centers. All of them have also developed their own special beauty.

Damascus, with its growing population of about one million, is the capital of Syria. It is a city whose white towers rise above the apricot, almond, fig, and pomegranate orchards that grow in the oasis surrounding the city. Alive with a great many business, religious, and cultural activities, it is a city with a variety of thoroughfares and architecture.

(10)

A city with a history that goes back several thousand years, Damascus is today the capital of Syria.

Modern buildings and factories as well as ancient monuments line the wide boulevards and narrow, winding streets. New sections, modern in style, are constantly under construction. But the older sections of Damascus still house the ancient Muslim, Christian, Armenian, and Jewish quarters. In contrast to the newer industrial plants, there are the traditional marketplaces and small workshops where people practice ancient arts and crafts. The goldsmiths, silversmiths, brassworkers, leatherworkers, and the weavers of fine damask cloth are everywhere in the marketplace, creating and selling their handicrafts.

No one knows exactly how old Damascus is. But we do know that it has existed since before the time of Abraham. It was ruled at one time or another by Egyptians. The Hittites who, it is believed, came out of Europe and crossed into Asia by way of the Aegean Sea, ruled Syria. So did the Israelites and the Aramaeans, who moved into Syria from the east about 1200 B.C. Assyrians, who ruled almost the entire known ancient world at one time, made Damascus one of their principal cities. Persians, Romans and Greeks were among others who occupied Damascus.

It was on the road to Damascus, that St. Paul was converted to Christianity. The Romans built a temple for their god Jupiter when they held the city. The Roman emperor Theodosius I, later, tore down the temple and built a magnificent church on its foundations, in A.D. 373. Three hundred years later, Arabs conquered the city and converted the church into a mosque. The Great Mosque, as it is still called, with its colored marbles and splendid mosaics, is still considered one of the most beautiful structures in the world.

After the Arabs' initial conquest of Damascus, others attacked and attempted to take the city. The Christian Crusaders failed, but the Egyptians, the Karmathians out of Yemen, and the Turks, among others, were more successful.

Almost all those who conquered the ancient city left their marks, and these may be read in the varied architecture of Damascus and in the nature of its population. The major city in the Syrian Arab Republic, Damascus is also one of the most interesting cities in the world.

ALEPPO

Aleppo, with its population of about 600,000, is Syria's second largest city and also the country's most important industrial and commercial city. It is a principal railway junction, linked by road to Latakia, Syria's principal oil seaport.

One of the most modern cities in the Middle East, Aleppo has many broad streets and modern office and apartment buildings. But like Damascus, it has its ancient quarters with old houses on narrow and twisting lanes.

Aleppo's chief marketplace, the largest such marketplace in the world, stretches through 15 miles (24 km) of winding streets and covered alleyways. There are also old warehouses to which camel caravans laden with goods have for centuries brought merchandise later to be sold at the marketplace.

HOMS

Homs is the third largest industrial city in Syria. It is situated on a broad highway on which the original milestones, built during the Roman occupation of the city, are still plainly visible.

Muslims built the famed Khaled Ibn al-Walid mosque in

Above: the ancient city of Aleppo has over the years survived numerous invasions by foreign conquerors. This view of Aleppo shows the citadel, or fortress, built in the twelfth century. Right: these ruins are found in Palmyra, a city that flourished as an oasis on the trade route across Syria as long ago as the first century B.C.

Homs. The Christian Crusaders built a most extraordinary castle just 40 miles (64 km) outside the city. Homs is also the home of many ancient churches including the church in which, it is said, a belt of the Holy Virgin was found.

Today Homs is a busy communications area. It lies on the trade route from Damascus to Aleppo and connects central Syria with the port of Tartus on the Mediterranean Sea. It also produces much that is essential for the country's economy in its electric plants, oil refineries, and fertilizer factories.

HAMA

Hama, the fourth of Syria's largest cities, is the country's most important grain area. It is noted throughout the world, as well as in Syria, for its fabulous *noria* (waterwheels). These waterwheels are giant in size, some 80 feet (24 m) in diameter, and are used to bring up water from the Orontes Rivers. It is this water from the Orontes that irrigates the farmlands in the Hama region and makes them so productive.

There were other great cities in ancient Syria, among them Palmyra, an oasis north of the Syrian desert. Time has turned much of their great structures into ruins, but archeologists continue to uncover the great monuments of Syria's fascinating past. Today, the government of Syria helps to preserve and even to restore many of these relics.

The larger cities of Syria may be up-to-date, with modern buildings and broad streets, but their ancient heritage continues to live in their winding alleyways and in their marketplaces as well as in the ruins that dot their landscape.

THE PEOPLE
OF SYRIA

Syria is a land of many minorities, many languages, and many religions. In its long history many different peoples from many different lands invaded Syria. Some came peacefully from the north of Europe and Asia to make their homes in a warmer climate. Many came to take advantage of the trade routes of Syria, and these traders stayed on.

The Persians conquered Syria in 539 B.C. In 333 B.C., Alexander the Great conquered Syria. For a thousand years, until the Arabs conquered the land in A.D. 636, Syria lived under Greek or Roman control. During this thousand years, a great number of Greeks, Italians, and other Mediterranean people, migrated to Syria and made it their home.

Two farmers walk before an irrigation ditch designed to bring water to the dry fields behind them.

The Arabs, nevertheless, are the great majority among the peoples living in Syria. The vast majority among these Syrian Arabs are Muslims though some are Christians. Almost all Arabs in Syria speak Arabic.

Today there are three forms of the Arabic language. There is the classical Arabic of the Koran, the sacred book of the Muslims. There is the literary Modern Standard Arabic. And there is the spoken language called Syrian Arabic. Only students and scholars of the Koran can understand classical Arabic. Educated Syrians speak both Modern Standard Arabic and Syrian Arabic. The un-educated Syrians — and they are in the great majority — understand Modern Standard Arabic, though they cannot speak it.

EMPLOYMENT

About 60 percent of the entire Syrian population work on farms or at breeding animals. Their farms produce wheat, barley, peas, sugar beets, and garden vegetables as well as cotton and tobacco, fruits and nuts. The animals the Syrians breed are mostly sheep, goats, horses, mules, donkeys, and camels.

About 9 percent of the Syrian people work in medium- to large-sized industries. They spin and weave cloth and work in the food-processing plants and the grain mills as well as in the sugar and oil refineries. They also work in cigarette factories and in factories that manufacture chemical products. They make tele-visions, refrigerators, and furniture too.

Another 9 percent of the Syrian population work in trans-portation. They run the buses and trains, keeping them in good repair.

About 10 percent of the Syrian population work as officials

of one kind or another in the government structure and in the armed forces.

There is one thing lacking in this Syrian working class. Syria badly needs more people with managerial skills, people who can run its growing economy with the best kind of planning and with the efficiency that it calls for.

THE MINORITIES

The Kurds, about 6 percent of the Syrian population, have their own language, which is closely related to Persian, the major language in Iran. They are a tribal people and are fiercely independent. Many came from Turkey between 1924 and 1938 when they were persecuted by the Turks.

Some Kurds live in the Syrian cities and have achieved positions of supervisors and foremen. Others are nomads, tending to their flocks of sheep and goats. Most Kurds, however, are farmers and have settled in the foothills of the Taurus Mountains north of Aleppo and in the Jazira region.

Three percent of the Syrian population is Armenian. While a number of Armenians, like the Kurds, have lived in Syria for

Some Syrian women living
in cities still wear
the traditional costume,
though most have
given it up in favor of
contemporary Western dress.

generations, most of them arrived as refugees, escaping persecution by the Turks between 1925 and 1945.

Among the other and smaller minorities in Syria are the Turkomans, the Circassians, the Assyrians, and the Jews.

The Turkomans came to Syria from central Asia. Originally nomads, most Turkomans have taken on the habits, the dress, the customs, and the language of the Arabs. Many of them, however, still speak their own Turkic language and maintain their traditional customs.

The Circassians, like the Turkomans, were originally nomads. They came to Syria after the Russians conquered their homeland between the Black and Caspian seas in the nineteenth century. Circassians still tend to their grazing of horses, cattle, sheep, and goats, as did their ancestors. But they have become good farmers, too, particularly with the growing of wheat. Like the Turkomans, the Circassians are Muslims.

There are about fifteen thousand Assyrians in Syria. They live in about twenty villages in the Khabur River area. They are small-scale farmers, and, though their land is irrigated, they do not make more than a bare living out of their farms. They speak Syriac, a form of the ancient Aramaic language, which is closely related to Hebrew. Syriac was the language of this entire Mideastern region before the language of the Arabs took over.

JEWS IN SYRIA

The Jews have lived in Syria for centuries. At one time there were some thirty thousand Jews in Syria. The conflict between Syria and Israel has driven most of them out of the country. At present there are no more than about four thousand Jews who have remained.

At one time there was a fairly prosperous community of Jews in Aleppo who were an important part of the city's commercial life. Now the few Jews who have remained there are poor, living in the Bab al Fraj, a run-down area in the middle of the town.

The story is much the same for the Jews who live in Damascus. A few important professionals, mainly doctors, still have their homes in the capital city. Others are mostly peddlers, shopkeepers, and craftspeople.

Minorities in Syria live in compact groups, almost closed communities. The loyalty of these minorities is first toward their communities. It is in fact almost a tribal loyalty.

TOWNS, VILLAGES, AND TRIBES

Until the mid-1960s the most powerful people in Syria were its wealthy landowners and industrialists. The landowners, for the most part, had inherited their wealth. The industrialists had made all their money with the developing industries in the country.

Another important group were the religious teachers and the judges (*kadis*) and interpreters (*muftis*) of Islamic law. Generally, this group supported the landowners and the industrialists, and both groups lived in and exercised their power from the big cities and towns.

TOWNS

Craftspeople, traders, and the working class living in the towns and cities had very little to say about the running of the country.

Villagers and tribespeople had practically no power at all. It was the professionals, the technicians, and especially people connected with the military who became the most powerful people in Syria during the 1960s.

Power has changed hands in Syria, but the change has not altered the traditional differences between Syrian towns and villages or between those who live in the villages and those who live in Syrian tribes.

The people of each of these separate groupings look upon each other as socially different. They keep a distance between each other through their different customs and life-styles. They wear different clothes and eat different kinds of food. They furnish their homes differently and speak the Syrian language with different accents. Marriage between town, village, and tribal families is still very rare. Each group is careful to maintain its differences from the other groups.

About one-third of Syria's population lives in its towns and cities, and almost 70 percent of these people live in Damascus and Aleppo. Those families who have lived in the towns for perhaps centuries generally live in the heart of the town. Some live in houses that were built before the Greeks and Romans conquered Syria. There is usually a marketplace of considerable size in every Syrian town.

In the towns, as in the cities, people of different national origin and of different religions tend to live in separate areas. Many of these areas have their own church, synagogue, or mosque. All have shops that serve the special needs of its community in terms of food and clothing. All have their own coffee shops where men meet for social and business reasons. (Women, with very little exception, are still kept apart from the men's world.)

A land of contrasts, a land of change —
a shepherd walks his flock alongside a
new hydroelectric project on the Euphrates River.

In the towns, Syrians have begun to dress more and more in the style of the Western European countries. The traditional burnoose (the Arab cloak and hood) has, however, not altogether disappeared from the town streets, shops, cafés, and marketplaces.

There has been one more break with tradition among townspeople. Syrians, moving into the newest sections of the city and its suburbs, choose to live among people of their own economic position rather than among those of their faith or ethnic background.

VILLAGE LIFE

People who live in the villages are for the most part farmers. The village, in addition, will often have a small storekeeper, someone who runs the coffee house, and a barber.

Generally, the entire village will belong to the same faith. Sometimes an entire village will have descended from a single ancestor, the founder of the village. Where there are several families in the village, each family will tend to live in a section of its own. The heads of these families, usually old and middle-aged men, are the leaders of the village. They meet in the coffee house to discuss whatever problems the village may have. It is in the coffee house, too, that they make all the decisions that affect their village life.

The traditional head of the village is its *mukhtar*. He is not necessarily its most respected citizen. Most often he is chosen mukhtar only because of his ability to read and write Arabic.

This practice, however, like so many other Syrian traditions, is undergoing a change. More and more of the village children attend school. More and more of them travel to the towns for their high school education. As a result, more and more villagers can read and write and are eligible for the post of mukhtar.

In recent years the very distinct separation of the village from the town has become less and less rigid. More and more, villagers are making trips to their nearby towns, made possible by improved roads and public buses. Villagers go to town more frequently to do their marketing and also go for medical care, entertainment, and, often, for business reasons.

Many of the young people who attend the high schools in towns choose to stay and live there after they have finished their education. Others leave the farms to find jobs in the towns. Still, the village remains an important part of the Syrian way of life, and of its economy.

TRIBAL LIFE: A CHANGING CULTURE

In the mid-1960s the tribal population of Syria was about 7½ percent. It is less today for a number of reasons.

First, while the Syrian government appreciates the need for its shepherds, it frowns on the nomadic life of its Bedouin tribes. Slowly but certainly the government is settling the Bedouin tribes in the villages where they can be better controlled as well as educated. Second, the government has extended its law into the desert where it had never been before.

Third, the number of new roads in the deserts, and the cars, buses, and trucks that ride them, have cut deeply into the grazing lands of the nomads.

Still, there are eight nomadic tribes who roam the Syrian deserts. Each of the tribes is said to have descended from a common male ancestor and is named after him. Each tribe is therefore made up of a number of related bands of nomads. Prestige, among the men of the tribe, is measured not by a male's ability to read or write. If a tribesman is to be respected, it must be because of his ability to ride a horse and hunt, and to herd animals, handle men, and settle disputes among his fellow tribesmen. He is also respected for the size of his flocks and especially for the number of horses he owns.

The mukhtar of each band of tribespeople is more respected than the mukhtar of the village. He is generally the most important member of his family and the leader of his nomadic band's tribal council. This tribal council is made up of the most respected members of the various families of the Bedouin tribal band.

The council meets every day in the guest house of the mukhtar to discuss whatever problems the band may have and to make decisions. It also hears the complaints and problems of individual men of of the tribe and tries to settle disputes between them.

If, in the case of a dispute, the council cannot arrive at a decision, it takes the dispute to a higher "judicial" body. This body is made up of a group of tribesmen whose power and prestige is higher than that of the band's mukhtar.

If this more important "judicial" body cannot arrive at a decision, the quarrel is taken to the sheikh of the entire tribe. He is the most respected member of the tribe and, for all purposes, its ruler, leader, and chief judge.

The government of Syria may consider the life of its nomads to be primitive, but the Bedouin, especially among those villages on the borders of the Syrian deserts, are still admired for their independence and pride.

THE FAMILY

Nothing is more important to the Syrian people than their families and their family life. The Syrians' loyalty to their family is greater than loyalty to the country, the flag, or anything else. And nothing is more important to Syrians than the dignity of the family.

Children are educated not to be independent, as they are in so many Western countries, but to be good members of the family. The Syrians consider a family to include not only the grandparents, parents, and children of the household but also all the uncles, cousins, and nephews who carry the family name. To be good members of the family, children are taught to respect their clan and to be loyal to it. They are taught to obey the wishes and will of their elders, particularly the wishes and will of their father. Syrian adults in their forties and fifties continue to obey their fathers and grandfathers.

Syrians who hold a public office, to which they have been elected or appointed, will choose cousins and other relations to staff the office. Syrians who run factories, shops, or any other business will hire their relations to work with them. Business firms are likely to deal with other business firms that are headed by one of their family.

WOMEN: A CHANGING ROLE

Traditionally, women in the Syrian family were officially regarded as beings of secondary importance. By tradition as well, they have taken no part in the business or political life of the country, have veiled their faces, and have had no contact at all with men to whom they were not related.

Traditions, however, give way to changing times. Today fewer and fewer women veil their faces. In the cities, and even in the towns and villages, women are beginning to enter the business world. In 1976 Syria's President Hafez al-Assad appointed a woman, Naja Attar, Minister of Culture and National Guidance. This was the first time in history that a woman held a post in Syria's presidential cabinet.

Still, for the great majority of women in Syria, their place is in the home. They cook, bake, sew, do some of the work on the farm, and give birth to children. If a woman is to be considered a good wife, she must give birth to sons. It is still not uncommon for a Syrian man to divorce his wife if she gives birth only to daughters.

Bedouin women usually marry before their fourteenth birthday. Women in the villages often marry between the ages of fourteen and eighteen. Only in the middle and upper classes of the towns and cities do women wait until they have reached their eighteenth birthday before they marry.

Marriages in Syria, with little exception, are arranged by the parents of the bride and groom. These are usually unions between families of equal social and economic position. Marriages within the family clan are preferred by the Syrians. They encourage, particularly, marriages between cousins.

Because marriages are arranged, often a bride and groom meet at the wedding ceremony for the first time. In any case, a Syrian man does not begin to court his future wife until after they have become engaged. He never sees her alone, even when he is courting her, but always among a group of friends — most likely to be members of the family clan.

By Islamic law, a Muslim man is allowed to have four wives. Sometimes he will marry a second wife when he and his first wife have not produced a son. But most Syrian men find it hard enough to provide financial support for a family with just one wife.

HOUSING

The Syrian family, usually of three generations, headed by grandfather, father, and son, will live under one roof. In the north-

Syrian women are slowly but surely assuming a greater role in the economy and welfare of their country.

(32)

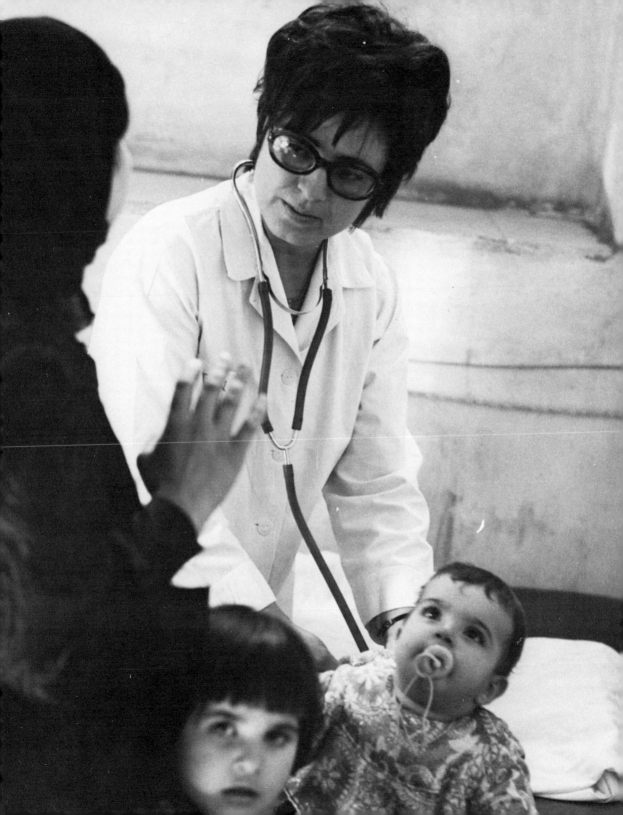

These homes outside the city of Aleppo
are made of clay, mud, and straw.

eastern areas of the country, its house will be beehive-shaped and made of mud and straw. In the southern and eastern regions of the country, the family will usually live in a house that has been built with stone blocks. The middle-class family, in the towns and cities, will generally live in an apartment made of cinder blocks and concrete. Wealthy families generally live in houses constructed with stone.

The Bedouin family lives in a felt tent, whether tending flocks in the summertime or cultivating a bit of land in the wintertime. The poorest families, mostly in towns and cities, find some unused piece of land and build shacks of hammered tin cans and corrugated iron in which to live.

FOOD

The diet of the Syrian family varies, too, according to its income and sometimes according to its way of life. Families who live in the villages get very little meat. When dinner is served, it consists mainly of rice, beans, yogurt, cheese, olives, squash, and peas. There might also be watermelon, figs, dates, or grapes for them to eat.

The Bedouin, whose work is mainly with sheep and goats, will naturally have more milk and meat to eat than do the villagers.

In the towns and cities, of course, the diet of a family will be more varied, depending on its income. Basically, however, rice, beans, yogurt, cheese, and the fruits of the country are the staples of the Syrian family wherever it lives and however it makes its living.

EDUCATION

For many years the traditional school in Syria was the *kuttab*. The kuttab is an ungraded religious school. It is usually housed in a mosque where the children study the teachings of the Muslim prophet Mohammed and memorize long passages from the Muslim holy book, the Koran. The children are also taught reading, writing, and simple arithmetic. For the most part, the kuttab has been replaced by secular (nonreligious) schools under government supervision. But the kuttab still exists in the poorer villages where government schools have yet to be built.

Government schools are free of charge, and children must attend primary school from the age of six until they are eleven. In the primary school, children are taught religion, Arabic grammar, composition, arithmetic, hygiene, history, geography, civics, handicrafts, physical education, and singing. In country schools, the children are also taught agricultural subjects in the later grades.

If Syria's young people wish to continue their education, they have to pass rigid examinations to get into the intermediate schools and then into the secondary schools. The openings in these schools are comparatively few, and only those with high grades have the opportunity for advanced education.

In the three-year intermediate schools, the children are taught religion, mathematics, history, geography, civics, general science, music, a foreign language (generally French), and physical education. In addition, the boys study agriculture, and the girls study home economics.

The three-year Syrian secondary schools are more specialized. After the first year, during which the students take general courses, the young people devote two years to either the humanities or the sciences. All male students in the secondary school must take military training in order to graduate.

The students with the best academic records may go on to the University of Damascus where they may study law, medicine, dentistry, engineering, science, fine arts, commerce, pharmacology, agriculture, Islamic jurisprudence, or education. Or they may go to the University of Aleppo to study engineering, science, agriculture, law, or medicine.

There are a number of private schools in Syria, most of them established by French missionaries. But all schools in Syria — primary, intermediate, secondary, or university and whether they are private schools or public schools — are closely supervised by the Syrian government.

The government sees to it that primary students learn the

*A reading lesson in a boys primary
school in the Euphrates Basin.*

stories of ancient and modern Arab heroes, that they study the ancient civilizations of Babylonia, Syria, and Egypt, and that they learn the duties of a Syrian citizen. In the intermediate and secondary schools the government encourages vocational studies. Syria needs technicians. Above all, the government demands the development of a strong national patriotism, an allegiance to both the country and its ruling Baath (Arab Socialist Resurrection) Party.

It should be noted that the school population in Syria is largely male. Only ten years ago there were twice as many boys as girls attending the schools. At the universities only about 17 percent were women. This situation is changing as more and more young Syrian women free themselves from the second-class traditions they suffered for centuries, and prepare themselves for a productive role in their society through education.

RELIGION

Syria is a Muslim country. Only 13 percent of its people are Christians. Half of one percent are Jewish, Yezidi, and others. But the vast majority of the population — over 85 percent — are followers of Islam. It is a religion that came into being at the beginning of the seventh century and spread not only among Arabs but throughout the world. There are even Muslim sects in the United States. Islam is the religion whose god, in Arabic, is called Allah. Mohammed, Muslims believe, was Allah's prophet.

According to the teaching of Islam, in A.D. 610 an Arab merchant named Mohammed in Mecca, Saudi Arabia, received a call from Allah to preach a new message. These messages from Allah to the prophet Mohammed were recorded in a sacred book, the Koran. The Koran prescribes a way of life for faithful Muslims.

Everything Muslims do or think, in or out of a house of worship (the mosque), is governed by the writings of the Koran.

THE FIVE PILLARS OF FAITH

There are five main principles, or "pillars of faith," each Muslim must follow:

1.   At least once in their lifetime, all Muslims must say, "There is no god but Allah, and Mohammed is his prophet."

2.   All Muslims must pray five times a day: at dawn, at noon, in the mid-afternoon, at sunset, and after nightfall. They wash themselves before they pray, cover their heads, take off their shoes, and kneel on a carpet. They always face Mecca, the birthplace of Mohammed, as they pray, and they prostrate themselves continually until their prayers are done.

3.   All Muslims must be charitable to the poor.

4.   Except if they are physically weak, sick, or soldiers, Muslims must keep the fast of Ramadan. Ramadan is the ninth month in the Muslim calender, the month in which the Koran was sent down by Allah. During Ramadan, according to Muslim belief, the gates of Paradise are open, the gates of hell shut, and the devils in chains. During this entire month, the faithful must fast from sunrise until the dark of evening.

5.   Once in their lifetime, if possible, Muslims must make a pilgrimage *(hajj)* to Mecca.

When Muslims are called to prayer by the *imam* (a very important person in his community), they do not ask Allah for gifts. Muslims pray only to express their thanksgiving and adoration of God. There are no priests in Islam.

The Koran, like the Bible, calls on the faithful not to sin. It is a sin for Muslims to eat pork or drink alcoholic beverages. Other sins are much like those of Christians and Jews.

Islam has two major holidays. Each lasts for three or four days during which people wear their best clothes, go visiting, and give gifts to their friends and relatives. Id al-Adha is one of those holidays; the other is the most joyous holiday in the Muslim calendar, Id al-Fitr. It celebrates the end of the fast of Ramadan.

One interesting note about the faith of Islam is its relation with the Jewish and Christian faiths. According to the Koran, Abraham, the father of Israel, was the first Muslim. Jesus Christ, it is believed by Muslims as well as Christians, was the child of the Virgin Mary. Muslims believe that Jesus was not crucified but taken away by God, who left a shadow in his place. Jesus, they believe, will return one day at the end of the world. They believe that Mohammed, not Jesus, was God's last prophet.

Like other faiths, Islam is made up of a number of sects. The great majority of Muslims in Syria belong to the Sunni sect. The second largest group of Syrian Muslims are Shiites, who are then split up into a number of smaller sects. The Ismailians, the Alawites, and the Druzes are offshoots of Shiism.

Most Syrians follow the teachings of Islam, which states that they must pray five times each day. This mosque was built in Damascus in 715.

(42)

A Christian church at an oasis in the Syrian desert

Islam permeates the life of all but the most sophisticated Syrian Muslims. Though they do not pray to Allah for help or gifts, they expect Allah's aid in troubled times, or in the resolution of problems, or in the successful attaining of some goal.

Christians in Syria are divided into five main sects. Some are Roman Catholics, and others are Protestants of various denominations. The vast majority of Syrian Christians, however, are Greek Orthodox, Uniat, and Nestorian. There were Christians in Syria long before Islam made its way into the country. Some of the first Christian communities in the history of the church were founded in and around Damascus.

Jews have lived in Syria since biblical times. David, king of ancient Israel, sent his victorious armies into Damascus. Hama (called Hamath in the Bible) was a city in ancient Israel. In 1492, during the Spanish Inquisition, when so many people were tortured and burned at the stake for their faith, Spain ordered all its Jews out of the country. Many of these Jews made their new home in Syria, where some of their descendents still live.

ROAD TO FREEDOM, ROAD TO WAR

For more than three thousand years, almost from the beginning of its history, Syria suffered a continual invasion of foreign peoples and was controlled by foreign powers. Phoenicians, Hittites, Hebrews, Assyrians, Egyptians, and Persians controlled parts or the whole of Syria in the distant past. The Greeks, Romans, Turks, and Christian Crusaders came later. In 1516 the Turks again conquered Syria, and for more than four hundred years Syria was part of the Turkish Ottoman Empire.

During the First World War, in September 1918, the British took Damascus, ousted the Turks, and set up an Arab government with Faisal ibn al-Husain at its head. The first Arab government in the Mideast in centuries, it did not last long.

A Syrian national congress proclaimed Faisal king in 1920,

but before the end of that year the French marched into Damascus and forced Faisal to abdicate, or give up, his throne. The short-lived Arab state ceased to exist. The French had been given a mandate over Syria by the League of Nations, and they intended to rule — by force if necessary.

FRENCH RULE

Arab nationalism, the battle for self-determination and self-rule, had begun to take shape more or less peacefully in the early 1800s. Under the French mandate, however, Arab nationalists began to take to violence and rebellion to attain their freedom from foreign domination.

The Druzes, a Muslim sect living in the region southeast of Damascus, rose in rebellion against the French in the summer of 1925. Although the French had a large army in Syria, it took them a full year to put down the rising. They were never able, however, to quiet the determination of the Arabs for self-government and a free Syria.

When France was overrun by the Germans in the Second World War, the Vichy French (collaborators with the Nazis) took control of Syria. But British and Free French troops were quick to oust the Vichy government in Damascus, and the administration of Syria was taken over by a Free French government.

The French had promised the Syrians independence. They were very slow, however, in delivering their promise. French troops were still in control of the country, and French officials were in control of much of its government when, in 1944, the Soviet Union recognized Syria as an independent state. In 1945 Britain gave Syria the same recognition.

Syrians were restless under this continued French military occupation. There was street fighting and bloodshed in Damascus and Aleppo. The French bombed and machine-gunned Damascus. There was serious fighting between the Syrians and the French in Homs and Hama. The British warned that they would intervene and reestablish order in the country. Winston Churchill threatened to send British troops into Syria, and Charles de Gaulle ordered his French troops to cease fire. It was not until February 1946, when the United Nations ordered the French to evacuate their troops from Syria, that the French armies began to leave Syrian soil. By April 17 of that year, all foreign troops had departed from Syria, and the Syrians, for the first time in several centuries, were at last in full control of their own country.

INDEPENDENCE

Syria, at last, was independent. But independence does not always mean peace. With independence, the unity with which all Syrians had fought for freedom was broken. In place of the unity, there arose within the country a struggle for power.

Politicians fought over the kind of government Syria should have. Villages fought against towns and cities for political leadership. The younger generation confronted the older and more religious people in the country. Damascus fought against Aleppo for political control. The various tribes pledged their loyalty to their tribal leaders. The Alawites actually attempted rebellion to achieve their own self-government.

The first government of free Syria was a republic under the presidency of Shukri al-Kuwatly. But Kuwatly's parliament was made up of every shade of Syrian thought and plan for action. It could not focus enough to effectively lead the country through its many problems.

Trouble between Israel and the Arab countries had been brewing for some time and continues to plague the entire Middle East up to the present day. The core of the trouble is a small strip of land, most of which lies between the Mediterranean Sea and the Jordan River. It was part of what was once called Palestine. Today it is Israel.

Israel became an independent nation in 1948, but Syria, Saudi Arabia, Iraq, Iran, Kuwait, Libya, and the other members of the Arab League have refused to officially recognize the existence of Israel. The Arab League, organized in 1945 to further the interests of the Arab world, maintains that Palestine belongs to the Palestinian Arab Muslims and not to Israeli Jews.

The claims of both Arabs and Israelis are made with a certain historical logic. Palestine is the Holy Land for both Muslims and Jews. It is the Holy Land for Christians, too. Palestine was the home of Jesus Christ. It is a place for Christian as well as Jewish and Muslim pilgrimage.

According to the Bible, Palestine is the land God promised to the children of Israel. It was the kingdom of Israel under King David, about 1,000 B.C. Almost nine hundred years later, after this kingdom had been destroyed by Assyrians and Babylonians, it again became a kingdom under the Maccabees, a dynasty of Jewish patriots. This kingdom lasted for seventy years until it was destroyed by the Romans, who expelled most of its Jewish population.

In A.D. 640, the Muslims overran Palestine, and Palestine

became part of the Arab world. It wasn't until some twelve hundred years later, about 1870, that Jews in any number began to return to Zion (the City of David) and Palestine.

The Jewish people never forgot the promise of the Lord. Their number in Palestine grew as they purchased land from the Palestinian Arabs and settled into colonies.

In 1917 Lord Balfour, Britain's foreign minister, promised to establish a Jewish "national home" in Palestine — with due regard for the non-Jewish Palestinians. This was during World War I when Britain was fighting against the Turks, who held Palestine at the time.

Lord Balfour's intentions were good and, under British control after the war, there was for a while the semblance of peace between the Arab and Jewish populations of Palestine. The peace did not last very long. In 1928 Arabs, who were opposed to the growing number of Jews in the land and to their purchasing of more and more Arab soil, attacked the Jews at the Wailing Wall in Jerusalem. The Wailing Wall, said to be a remnant of the temple King Solomon built, is sacred to the Jewish people. This was the beginning of the long conflict between Jews and Arabs.

When Hitler came to power in 1933, Jewish migration from Germany to Palestine increased greatly. So did the conflict between Arabs and Jews. There were attacks on Jews in the cities and, particularly, in their agricultural settlements.

The British tried to stop the fighting. There were plans to separate Palestine into two divisions, one Arab, the other Jewish. The Arabs would have nothing to do with such plans.

There was a lull in the fighting between Arabs and Jews

during World War II, but it grew worse in the years immediately after the war.

In 1948 the British withdrew all their troops, and Israel declared itself a sovereign state. Now the fighting between Arabs and Jews broke out in earnest. In May 1948 Syria, along with other Arab countries, invaded Israel, and its armies were defeated.

The defeat of Syria's armies in this first war against Israel deepened the Syrians' dissatisfaction with their government. On March 30, 1949, Brigadier General Husni al Za'im army chief of staff, ousted the government in power and, as the only candidate on the ballot, was elected president of the country.

He did not last long. Only 4½ months after he had assumed his powers, he was removed from office by another army coup. There were many more army coups to follow.

In 1958, in an effort to develop some stability within the country, Syria joined Egypt to create the United Arab Republic, under the presidency of Egypt's Gamal Abdel Nasser. This did not last too long either. Syria became an independent state once more in 1961.

ASSAD

Since 1970, following another military coup, General Hafez al-Assad has headed the Syrian government. While, since 1973, Syria has had a "People's Assembly" of 186 members, the effective powers of government are all held by Assad with the full support of his army.

Assad's most notable achievement in his efforts to strengthen the economy of Syria has been the completion of the 2½-mile- (4-km-) long Tabqa Dam on the Euphrates River. He has also introduced new varieties of wheat and fertilizers so that, for the first time, Syria has become an exporter of grain.

While Syria produces less than 3/10 of one percent of the world's production of oil, it has a number of pipelines that carry petroleum from the oil-producing countries to its ports on the Mediterranean. It is from these ports that oil is exported abroad. The oil pipelines bring much needed revenues to the Syrian government.

SYRIA AND ISRAEL

Syria has gone to war against Israel four times, beginning with the War of 1948. Each time the Syrian forces have been defeated. In the 1967 War, Syria lost its Golan Heights, a militarily strategic stretch of land, to Israel. The loss served only to deepen Syria's hostility toward Israel. Assad continues to encourage and aid guerrilla attacks on Israel and its people.

The Arab guerrilla forces operating against Israel are called the fedayeen. They were organized in the early 1950s and often use both Syria and Jordan as training grounds. They operate in

Syrian President Hafez al-Assad gives President Jimmy Carter a warm handshake during President Carter's visit to Syria in 1977.

small bands, relying on surprise raids for their success. They operate within Israel itself, ambushing buses and bombing shops, marketplaces, and hotels; or they swoop out of a nearby country (often Lebanon) to attack some outlying Israeli village or agricultural complex.

The anti-Israeli guerrillas are mostly Palestinian Arabs, Arabs who left Palestine when it was declared Israeli territory in 1948. However, a good number of Jordanians and Syrians may be counted in their ranks.

Syria wholeheartedly aids the fedayeen and the cause of the hundreds of thousands of Palestinian refugees now encamped in Syria and Jordan. In fact, Syria has been the most ardent supporter of the fedayeen. With the backing of the refugees and most of the Arab world, they would like to drive the Israelis out of the Middle East and return Palestine to the Arab Palestinians. When in 1977 President Anwar el-Sadat of Egypt unofficially recognized Israel as a sovereign state and proposed a peace between the two countries, Assad accused him of betraying the Arab people.

In February 1978 Assad, in a one-party election, was reelected President of Syria. He is the first Syrian president to serve a full seven-year term since the country became independent in 1946. His election by an overwhelming vote was judged to be a vote of confidence in Syria's opposition to peace with Israel.

The Syrians are a militant people. Their country may be poor, but they have powerful allies. They are backed by the Soviet Union. And it was the oil-rich Arab countries of Saudi Arabia, Iran, Libya, and others who stopped the shipment of their oil to the United States and other Western powers friendly to Israel during Syria's 1973 war against the Israelis. It was a boycott that practically crippled the economies of most Western nations.

The 1973 War was not won. Nor was it lost. And Syria is still determined that the Middle East will one day be all Arab.

FOR FURTHER READING

Caldwell, John C. *Let's Visit the Middle East*. New York: John Day, 1972.

Copeland, Paul W. *The Land and People of Syria*. New York: Lippincott, 1972.

Hodgkin, E. C. *The Arabs*. New York: Viking Press, 1975.

Peretz, Don. *The Middle East*. Boston: Houghton Mifflin, 1973.

INDEX

ABOUT THE AUTHOR

Henry Gilfond is the author
of several Franklin Watts
books for young adults
including *Voodoo*, *Genealogy*,
and *The New Ice Age*. He has
also written extensively
for television and theater.

Mr. Gilfond and his wife Edythe
live in New York City and
Shinnecock Hills, New York.

DATE DUE			